I0469493

Learn The Stock Market

Learning the Basics to Trading

Gary Duvalle

One of the very nice things about investing in the stock market is that you learn about all different aspects of the economy. It's your window into a very large world.
- Ron Chernow

I'm involved in the stock market, which is fun and, sometimes, very painful.
- Regis Philbin

Copyright 2013 JK Publishing

All rights reserved. No part of this book may be reproduced by any means whatsoever without the written permission from the author, except brief portions quoted for purpose of review.

All information in this book has been carefully researched and checked for factual accuracy. However, the author and publisher make no warranty, express or implied, that the information contained herein is appropriate for every individual, situation, or purpose, and assumes no responsibility for errors or omissions. The reader assumes the risk and full responsibility for all actions, and the author will not be held responsible for any loss or damage, whether consequential, incidental, special or otherwise that may result from the information presented in this publication.

Table Of Contents

The Basics Of Stock Trading: A Simple Guide

The idea of stock trading is something that overwhelms and confuses many people simply because they do not understand how the process works. Some people have a natural gift for trading stocks, so they naturally excel in this department. For most people, however, trading stocks is a bit of a mystery. It is considered something magical that happens amidst a crowded room of yelling people. All of a sudden, you own a small portion of a company and the success of your investment is now completely dependent upon that company's ability to turn a profit. This is a somewhat accurate depiction of what trading is, but let's try to make things a little bit clearer.

An Explanation Of Stocks

To put it simply, stocks are a method for companies to generate some investment capital. In other words, they offer shares of their company's future profitability in return for some upfront investment capital. This arrangement works out well for both the company and the investor. The company receives much needed revenue, and the stockholder not only receives dividends from the company's future profits, but they also have the opportunity to influence the company's direction.

The Stock Trading Process

Today, there are two ways that stocks can be traded. They can either be traded electronically or using the traditional floor exchange. Naturally, today's technology has prompted a push towards electronic trading. Surprisingly however, floor trading still remains as the most popular way to trade stocks. These two methods follow the same principles, but the process in which they are executed differs.

Floor Exchange: When people hear the term "floor trading", images from movies and television shows about Wall Street tend to pop up. Most people picture hundreds of stock brokers running around a room frantically shouting at each other. It would seem as if this is the way the stock market functions day in and day out. Let's say you wanted to purchase 150 shares of Company X. Once you notify your broker that this is what you want, they will get in touch with the floor clerk. The floor clerk will already know who is looking to sell 150 shares of Company X. A price is then agreed upon and communicated to you. Once the transaction is complete, you will receive a confirmation letter in the mail. At this point, you officially own a portion of Company X.

Electronic Exchange: Electronic trading is similar in nature. The only difference is that the buyer and the seller are brought together via online. The transactions are also immediate. Instead of working with a broker over the telephone, an electronic broker will oversee the trading. This actually puts you closer to the trading floor than the traditional floor exchange method. Of course, this does not mean that you are actually trading on the floor of the stock exchange yourself. You will still need to work with a broker, who will handle all of the transactions. It does not matter how small your shares of stocks are, you still obtain some ownership of the company.

Why Bother Trading Stocks?

Just as there are thousands of stock trades that happen each day, there are thousands of reasons to start trading. There are many people that trade because they are looking for financial gain. However, there are also some people that just enjoy the whole process and want to participate in the market economy. There is also a great deal to be learned from trading stocks as you have the opportunity to really see how the government handles commodity regulation. Trading stocks is also a great way to learn how successful companies develop and grow.

Why are you attracted to the idea of trading stocks? Maybe you like the idea of being able to own a portion of a company, or maybe you just enjoy the process. Stock trading can also be an excellent secondary income source. If your investments pan out, they can actually become your sole source of income if you choose.

If trading is something that interests you, start paying close attention to the markets. Check out some of the major newspaper publications or look online. Test out the process by making imaginary investments. You can track your investments and go through the motions before you actually take the plunge and make a real investment. Once you are comfortable with your skills and knowledge, you will feel much better about turning your pretend investments into real ones. Do not be afraid to take it slow and watch the markets closely. Of course, the most important rule of all is to have fun with it!

Understanding The Major Stock Indexes

There are quite a few different stock indexes and it is important to remember that each one is different. These indexes are often cited by financial services and news outlets as a means of benchmarking portfolio performances. Part of what makes these indexes confusing to newcomers is the fact that companies and stocks are able to move in and out of these indexes all the time. This is how experts measure certain market sectors. For example, you may buy shares of Company X from the NYSE (New York Stock Exchange), but it may wind up being listed on the DJIA (Dow Jones Industrial Average). That being said, it helps to understand what the different indexes are and what makes each one different.

The Dow Jones Industrial Average (DJIA)

The Dow Jones is actually one of the oldest market indexes in America with the Dow Jones Transportation Average being the only other index that dates it. This index consists of thirty large companies that are publicly owned. How is this list assembled? The editors at the Wall Street Journal are actually the ones who choose these companies each year. It is a tradition that is over one hundred years old and was started in 1896 by Charles Dow and his business partner Edward Jones.

It is easy to assume that the companies on this list are industrial-based, but this is not the case. Back when this index first emerged, this list consisted of the top eleven companies, which just so happened to be large industrial organizations. Considering the industrial revolution was taking place in the early 1900s, this makes a lot of sense. Times have changed since then, and industry is not the only top seat in the market anymore. However, the ranking still remains the same. The thirty companies that make up the DJIA are ones that have reached the top of their class, so to speak, in their industry.

NASDAQ

The NASDAQ index is where technology stocks reign supreme. This index works differently than Dow Jones as it takes into consideration the value of the market and the worth of the companies listed. There are five thousand companies that are listed on the NASDAQ and it is one of the most followed indexes in the United States. The NASDAQ index is considered a good indicator of the performance of technology based companies. Because many of these companies have factories or plants in other countries, it is no longer considered an exclusive U.S. index. The biggest complaint people have regarding the NASDAQ index is that it consists mainly of small companies. This tends to increase the volatility of the index depending on how the companies perform.

S&P 500

The S&P 500 stands for Standard & Poor 500 and is an index that is exclusive to the United States. This means that if a company is listed on this index and decides to move its companies overseas, they will be removed from the list and replaced with another company that is U.S. based. The stocks listed here are all large-cap common stocks and may be traded actively on either the NASDAQ or the NYSE (New York Stock Exchange). The S&P 500 is the second most followed index just behind the Dow. Many consider it to be the trend leader for the U.S. economy.

As you can see, these indexes tend to differ greatly in how they compile their lists. However, they are still rather similar at the end of the day. Only the investor can decide which index is the best match for their financial status and their personal beliefs. While you do not have to be as knowledgeable in the stock market as a broker would be, it still helps to at least know the basics.

Fundamental Analysis: What Is It? Why Do I Need It?

Through the use of fundamental analysis, traders attempt to predict a company's future. What the term is actually referring to is the economic status and overall health of the entity that is being analyzed. There are many different objectives used during an analysis and a wealth of information is needed in order to truly determine where a company stands. So, why would someone want to bother with fundamental analysis then? There are many different reasons, but let's first take a deeper look into what this method is.

Fundamental Analysis Explained

The fundamental analysis process can be quite complex and involves the analyzation of the company's financial statements, what type of management they have and how they measure up against their competition. When fundamental analysis is applied to futures and stocks, the focus is typically put on the company's revenue, economic demand for their products or services, interest rates and even production schedules. There are two basic ways to distinguish fundamental analysis from other types of analysis, like investment or technical.

With fundamental analysis, investors attempt to answer questions like:

- How does the company fare against their competition? Are they ahead of the game or barely getting by?
- Does the company turn a profit?
- Is the company's management attempting to hide parts of their books?
- Is the company in a position where they can pay their debts?

As you can imagine, there are literally hundreds of different questions you can answer using fundamental analysis. The goal is to get a picture of the fundamentals of the company, which includes the internal workings of the company and the demand for their products or services.

Objectives In Fundamental Analysis

To cover the main objectives of fundamental analysis, both current and historical company data are used. These objectives include:

- Price evolution predictions using the valuation of company stock
- Forecast the financial future of the company
- Determination of the company's credit risk
- Using business performance evaluations for predictions
- Evaluation of the company's management team and how they make business decisions internally

Using these objectives, business and stock analysts can learn a great deal about a company and their financial status without having to schedule a daily meeting with their accounting department.

Fundamental analysis makes use of both quantitative data, which is measured by numbers and qualitative data, which makes use of the characteristics or qualities of the company. Both qualitative and quantitative data must be used for fundamental analysis to truly be complete. The revenue and profits of the company are naturally important, but so are the ethics of the company and their brand strategies. Through this technique, the company as a whole is examined. Investing in the stock market requires that you know more than just the numbers. You should know the company you are investing in and ensure that their beliefs and practices are in line with yours.

Final Analysis

Those who use fundamental analysis will most certainly look at equations that correspond with company data. However, there are also other factors that are taken into consideration. These are the types of things that can only come with experience. Naturally, the company's financial statements will be an important part of the analysis. At the same time, having a good understanding of brand strategy trends and the decisions board members make will also have an influence on stock prices. These are all important to a person who relies on fundamental analysis. There are many Wall Street moguls that have chosen to either opt in or out of a trade based on these types of factors. The process is about more than just facts. It is about gut feelings as well.

Those who are new to stock trading may be a bit turned off by the amount of work that goes into evaluating a stock. However, there are a number of advantages to performing fundamental analysis. If done properly, it can guide you in the right direction and make the most out of your investment. It can also help save you money by avoiding bad trades. It is true that the most powerful stock traders use this analysis as their method to make money in the stock market, thus it only makes sense that you should use it as well.

Technical Analysis: Let's Talk Numbers

When you hear the term "technical analysis", what comes to mind? For some, they imagine a math whiz scribbling away at complex mathematical formulas. Others picture a person hunched over their computer in their cubicle crunching numbers. These are the stereotypical images of technical analysts, but the truth is that these individuals could very well be your neighbor next door or the quiet woman in the corner of the coffee shop. Let's take a deeper look at what technical analysis is and what kind of information it can offer.

The Basics Of Technical Analysis

A technical analyst is someone who focuses on trends and patterns in the markets. Once these trends and patterns have been recognized, the analyst will use them to make predictions about future trends. This is what they use to determine whether they will buy or sell a stock. Technical analysts rely greatly on the price chart. They study the chart very carefully and base many of their assumptions on it.

Technical analysis uses balance days, averages, support lines, flags, resistance and pennants to make predictions on price and volume. Other indicators are also used and typically come in the form of mathematical formulations. These are all used to determine whether or not an asset is trending and whether or not that trend is up or down.

Technical Analysis Objectives

The goal of technical analysis is to predict movements in price. This type of risk control is positive for long term returns. Technical analysts understand where the market is going and they can determine where the larger positive gains are so they can avoid the smaller gains or losses. If analysis is carried out properly, larger gains will clearly outweigh losses.

There are many different ways to carry out technical analysis as far as charting is concerned. Many traders combine numerous elements from these methods to make use of the best of each thought process. Technical analysis can be used to determine which stocks, indexes or markets will be most profitable for traders. It is impossible to know with certainty exactly how much a market will fall or rise, but analysts have a pretty good idea if the market will have a falling or rising pattern.

Final Analysis

Technical analysis is typically done in contrast to fundamental analysis. Whereas fundamental analysis relies greatly on information that is subjective, technical analysis makes use of objective information that companies either produce or display in the market. Technical analysts firmly believe that determining markets is merely a numbers game. Fundamental analysts, on the other hand, believe that data is important, but the company's managing practices and brand strategies are even more important.

Both of these analysis methods have their strengths and weaknesses. Neither one is right and neither one is wrong either. If you prefer to work with data and numbers, you might find that technical analysis is something you are better able to understand. This can be a very beneficial way to learn how to make wise investments in the stock market. Get as much information as you can and use this to your advantage.

The Truth About Day Trading

Many people have a skewed impression of what being a day trader is really like. They assume these individuals spend their day lazily looking over the daily stock charts and picking out stocks that look good to them. They press a few buttons on their laptops and then spend the rest of the day sitting by the pool. If this is your idea of a day trader, you are in for a rude awakening.

Day trading is not as simple and dry cut as you might have envisioned. It takes a great deal of knowledge and skill to be successful in this field. There is a lot of chart digging and panicking going on. A day trader is someone who buys and sells stocks at a rapid pace and they base their choices on how the market stands at the present moment. They do this with hopes that the stock will continue to climb for the short duration that the own the shares. Sometimes they trade within minutes and sometimes they trade within hours. Day trading can certainly be a risky business, but there are ways to avoid these risks.

How Risky Is Your Capital?

For the most part, day traders purchase stocks with borrowed money. This alone can be a major risk. In addition, they also trade with high speed and high intensity. They focus on the potential profits that may come from investing large amounts of money into stocks. At the same time, day traders must also realize that the combination of borrowed money and these intense trading practices come with a major risk for losses as well.

Day trading is not an illegal practice, but most investors do not have the means to really make money through day trading. It is not uncommon for the market to be quite volatile and day traders sometimes face devastating losses that the average person could not afford to sustain. Day traders need to be prepared to experience a severe financial loss at any given time. This is not to say that losses are something that happen to day traders all of the time or on a consistent basis. However, when they do suffer from losses, they are typically large amounts that have been invested initially.

Time Is Money

Day traders are technically not considered investors. Investors put their money into a stock long term and they keep a close eye on how the stock behaves over time. A day trader will buy and sell stocks within an hour, so they are not really investing per say. They spot trends and ride out the wave until it reaches its peak. At that point, they sell their shares. For this reason, day traders sell all of their stock before the day is through. There is far too much risk to hold onto them for that long as the price could greatly fluctuate.

A day trader spends a great deal of time in front of their computer during the day. If they want to at least break even, they must carefully watch the data ticker and the fluctuations of prices. At the same time, they must always be on the lookout for new trends. Just to keep up with the constant ups and downs of the market requires a great deal of concentration. Day traders must also have very powerful computers in order to keep up with the real time data flow. Needless to say, it is often difficult for day traders to break even with this type of investment. A successful day trader is always aware of the margin they must make before the close of the business day.

Determining The Risks

If you find this type of fast-paced, high intensity, high reward work to be enticing, day trading may be great for you. Keep in mind, however, that you must understand how to evaluate risks before you dive in. Although the rewards for a day trader are often quite high, the risks are equally as high. It is not uncommon for a day trader to just burn themselves out after a day of work.

It can be extremely difficult to maintain the level of concentration needed for day trading. Many who do this for a living have experienced sleepless nights worrying about how they are going to make up for their losses the next day. This can cause an extreme amount of stress even for the most experienced of traders.

Day trading should not be looked as a steady or stable business. You may experience some highs along the way, but you are likely to experience far more lows with day trading. If you are truly interested in getting into day trading, it is a wise choice to use your own money to minimize the risk. Make sure to take a few breaks so that you do not burn yourself out by the end of the day. It is also important for you to be able to recognize when you may be in too deep. Always be prepared to get out before the situation gets any worse.

Always remember that stock trading should be an enjoyable experience. Take your time, do some research and ask yourself some hard questions about whether or not day trading is really for you.

Penny Stocks: Are They Worth The Risk?

As the name suggests, penny stocks are stocks that are often traded for just pennies or a few dollars. To a newcomer, these stocks are very appealing. However, it is so important that you remember to do your research here. Everyone would love to invest in the next big company before it takes off, but the chances of this happening are quite slim. Generally speaking, companies that offer penny stocks offer very little information about their organization. There is also a lacking in standards, history and sometimes even ethics.

Not Enough Information

Companies that offer penny stocks are just making the transition from private to public, so it can be very difficult to find any information about them. Once a company goes public, they are then required by law to make all of their financial information, board member activities and a plethora of other data available to the public. When a company is private, they are not required to offer this kind of information. Right before going public, there are many companies that choose to provide the public with some information. The only problem with this is that you have no way of knowing whether or not this information is even true.

Unknown History

Because companies that offer penny stocks are just making the transition from a private company to a public company, they are putting their financial information out to the public for the first time. In other words, you have no history for which to compare this information. There is no real way to determine whether the information is correct or incorrect. Choosing to invest your money into a company without knowing their background or history is a great risk regardless of how little the investment is.

Fewer Regulations

Penny stocks are, naturally, not at the top of the charts. For this reason, the SEC has fewer regulations and standardizations in place. Companies that are lower on the charts do not have a minimum standard for stock fulfillment, so the data may be outdated because there is no real push to update reporting agencies. When companies can no longer hold their own on the major charts, they are sent back down to the lower charts in order to make room for a new company. This is why penny stocks can be a little bit deceiving. Not every company offering penny stocks is a new and up-and-coming company with the next big idea. This does not mean that all penny stocks are not trustworthy. It just means that they are a bit more risky as there are no standards involved.

An Ethics Problem
Naturally, smaller stocks will have a harder time getting investors to bite. Therefore, the price of the stock must continue to drop until it grabs someone's attention. There are also a number of people that buy a large amount of stock in an attempt to draw attention. Once investors see this trend and start to buy stock, the original buyers will sell them right away. All this does is inflate the price of the stock, and after a few months, the price once again drops because nothing happens. Unfortunately, this "scam-like" technique is completely legal.

The biggest issue with penny stocks is the lack of information. It can be very difficult to determine what the company's true financial standing is and what their real history looks like. Penny stocks are also lacking in the standards and ethics department. The price of penny stocks is often enticing, but investing in these stocks is quite risky. If you are not careful, it can have a detrimental effect on your financial situation.

Selling Stock: Using Logic And Intuition

The process of buying stock can be a fun and exciting one. You are choosing to invest your money into a company that you believe in and they appear to be doing great things. Although it can sometimes take a great deal of time and effort to find a stock worth investing in, there is no denying that the experience is quite rewarding.

Selling stock, on the other hand, is a completely different story. Investors typically feel a great deal of doubt and some apprehension before they sell. Sure, there is some apprehension and doubt when buying stock as well, but the excitement often keeps the situation positive. Choosing to sell stock is not an easy decision to make and is far from exciting. More often than not, however, it is usually in your best interest to sell.

Evaluating The Risks

If you find yourself contemplating whether or not this is the best time to sell the stock, then you have already made up your mind. The most difficult part of this process is determining whether or not you stand to gain any more money from holding onto the stock or lose a great deal more by sticking around. Before you even think about selling, you should weigh these risks carefully.

At this point, you are looking at two decisions that you need to take into consideration. Let's say the stock is going up and you decide to sell. Are you going to be okay with this decision regardless of what happens to the stock after you sell? On the other hand, if the stock is going down, are you going to be okay with your decision to just cut your losses? It helps to look a little deeper into each scenario so you can get an idea of why you should never be afraid to sell.

Highest Of Highs

It can be very exciting to see your stocks going up and doing well. Thoughts of the prospective income from this rise will no doubt cross your mind. However, it can be difficult to determine when the stock will finally reach its peak. People can make general predictions about stock trends, but there is no tried and true way to pinpoint when a stock will reach its peak. The best thing that you can do is establish all of the outcomes and choose the one that offers you the greatest comfort.

If is often recommended that when you sell your stock, you wash your hands of it. Do not go back to check on how well it is doing. If you have the compulsion to do this, then this is an indicator that you were not comfortable with your decision. You should have thought the decision out more thoroughly. Making the decision to sell means that you no longer care about the stock or the company's performance. If you look back, this means that you still care. Take the time to think your decision through first and then make the right one. This will help you avoid a lot of frustration later on down the road.

Lowest Of Lows
How would you feel if your stock went back up right after you sold it? Would you be devastated, or would you be okay with the idea of just cutting your losses? If you did decide to hold onto the stock, there is a chance that it will continue to decline. Are you going to be okay with the idea of riding out the low and taking the risk of losing even more money? Both sides of the coin need to be considered before you can really make a comfortable decision on whether or not to sell in a market that is declining.

By evaluating the risks and taking a look at all of the possibilities, you are better able to make an informed decision on whether or not it is a good idea to sell. It is, perhaps, even more important to consider how you are going to feel after you have made your decision. There is no doubting that the mere thought of selling your stock has already prompted you to start thinking about the financial repercussions of the decision. However, how you handle the aftermath is what will determine whether or not you made the right decision.

Using Charts To Buy Technology Stocks

Regardless of what type of stock you are considering purchasing, charts are a great way to identify stocks that are worthy of investment. While technology stocks are often the most valuable, they are also some of the most unpredictable stocks on the market. The prices of the raw materials that these companies use are in constant fluctuation, and new technology is constantly being developed. It is not uncommon for these stocks to rise rapidly and then fall quickly within the same day. The best way to analyze and evaluate these stocks is to use a chart.

Comparing Stocks

Charts can be used for a variety of different things, but they are especially useful for comparing and contrasting multiple technology stocks. The more stocks you are able to compare, the better idea you will have of how each company measures up to their competition. By using a chart, you will also know when companies are coming out with new products and how much press coverage they received for past product releases or newsworthy events.

Finding The Trends

If you use charts with technology stocks, you will find it much easier to pinpoint developing trends in the market. For example, if you see that software is trending upward, while semi-conductors are on the decline, you have a better idea of where to invest your money. You can take this one step further and compare raw commodity stocks alongside technology stocks to see how they affect their prices. Using the prior semi-conductor example, if you notice that each time the price of silicone increases, semiconductor stocks decline, you may be able to detect some early warning signs and be ready for what is to come.

Looking At The Bigger Picture

Remember that technology stocks often move around the charts. By keeping track of their movement, you can start to see the bigger picture. For example, you will learn which factors affect these stocks and how to predict what they will be doing next. All of the extensive data that you collect will help you to see the whole picture.

There are a number of reasons why stocks suddenly fluctuate, and these reasons are not always present when examining the company's new product launch or the prices of raw materials. Taking a closer look at what is going on in the world during the highs and lows will help you better predict which way the market will sway. Perhaps there was a large oil spill that caused the price of silicone to rise. This might cause the stocks of companies that use silicone in their products to rapidly decline as well.

Charts can provide you with a wealth of information regardless of which market you use them for; but they really shine when it comes to technology stocks. The sheer magnitude of information that you can obtain from technology charts will allow you to easily compare multiple stocks quickly and determine where trends are developing. This is an extremely useful tool to have when deciding which stocks to purchase. Not only will you have a clear picture of the company's overall health, but you will also be able to determine how healthy the market is as well. Through the use of technology charts, it has never been easier to start investing in technology stocks.

Buying China-Based Stocks Using Charts

When there are multiple factors that affect the prices of stocks, charts are typically the best tools to use. If you are considering investing in China-based stocks, it is important to keep in mind that political events, currency rates and the prices of exports and imports all affect the prices of stocks. Through the use of charts, you can look at each factor individually and then determine how it will affect the market as a whole. Let's take a closer look at how charts can be used for China-based stocks to look at these factors.

Currency Rates

The price of a stock may not really go anywhere within its own country's boarders, but there is still room to make a profit based on currencies. Because China has one of the cheapest currencies, using a chart to evaluate stocks makes the most sense. At this point in time, China fixes the value of their currency, the Yuan, against the U.S. currency, the dollar. This creates quite a bit of rivalry between the Chinese and American governments.

For example, take a look at the charts for stock that is based in China over the last five years or so. Between 2005 and 2008, the Yuan's value increased by nearly 22 percent. The Chinese government quickly put a stop to this, and since that time it has steadily risen three to five percent. It is estimated that the Yuan is actually undervalued by nearly 50 percent today, which means that China's economy is still expanding.

Future Trends

The United States has quite a few different indexes, including the S&P 500 and the Dow Jones Industrial Average. These indexes contain some of the biggest companies in the country. Outside of the US is the EAFE index, which stands for European, Australian, Far East. This is similar to the S&P 500. At the present moment, stocks that are based in China are not listed on the index.

Considering that China has one of the largest economies in the entire world, this is rather unusual. The problem is that China does not have enough securities to appear on the indexes. The country's tradeable volume is still very miniscule compared to the size of their overall economy.

In the coming years, China's market will continue to grow as will securities. Once this occurs, their share of the market will also grow until it reaches an appropriate size, which would equate to eighteen percent of the indexes. By using a chart, you can keep a close eye on this growth and determine when the best entry points are once China begins becoming more prominent in the market.

Those who are considering investing in stocks in China would greatly benefit from the use of charts. There is a plethora of information that you can obtain just by using currency to compare a number of different companies. You can also make comparisons based on company trends during a given length of time. A chart can provide a great deal of information about indexes or stocks that are not readily available using fundamental data.

If you are considering enriching your portfolio with China-based stocks, make sure that you use charts to compare companies. This is the best way to obtain reliable information and the best tool to find a smart entryway into this sometimes volatile market.

Avoid Panic By Studying Market Trends

The stock market can often be a rocky, volatile place. It is not uncommon for it to quickly raise and then plummet in just one day. Because the market is so unpredictable, it can be difficult to figure out what is going to happen next. This is why analysts learn to understand market trends as they offer some kind of consistency for traders. The current market trend can often be a good indicator of what the market will do in the coming days. It helps to know what the different types of trends are and what they can tell you about the current market conditions.

Upward Trend

One of the most important things that you must understand about markets, especially trends, is that you must always look at the long-term. It is common for stocks to rise and then fall at a rapid pace. These are often referred to as spikes. However, when you look over a long period of time, you see the bigger picture of whether the stock is trending upward or downward.

In order to know how long you should keep your money in the market, you need to understand time frame trends. For instance, if you see that that a particular stock has been steadily raising over a period of six years, you should expect to keep your money in that stock for at least six years. It is easy to panic when the market suddenly drops, but when you looked at the six year trend, the stock wound up coming back up at a much higher price in the end.

Downward Trend

Should a market begin trending down, or fall, there are still things that need to be taken into consideration. In fact, there may even be a hidden opportunity to gain from this downward trend. If the market is declining, you have the chance to sell off your shares and then buy more at a much lower price. This will allow you to experience a quicker gain when the market stabilizes once again.

Another thing to keep in mind is that there has always been a positive trend throughout the history of the stock market. In other words, even after a devastating period like the Great Depression, the market will return and begin trending upward once again. It always returns to the same level or higher than when the decline first appeared.

Why Track Trends?

When investing in the stock market, it is crucial that you pay very close attention to the trend of the market. This will give you an idea of how long you need to keep your money in the market in order to see a return and also what you should do with your stocks. During an upward trend, it is important to remain focused on the investment length and ignore any spikes that may occur. During a downward trend, it is best to use this situation to your advantage by selling and buying more stocks at an even lower price. This will provide you with quicker gains down the road.

Savvy stock investors are well aware of the importance of market trends and they use this valuable information to their advantage. This is equally important for beginner investors to learn simply because it helps avoid panic. When you understand how trends work and what the best course of action to take is, you are less likely to make a poor decision when you finally decide to purchase or sell your stock.

www.ingramcontent.com/pod-product-compliance
Lightning Source LLC
Chambersburg PA
CBHW051422170526
45165CB00004BA/1929